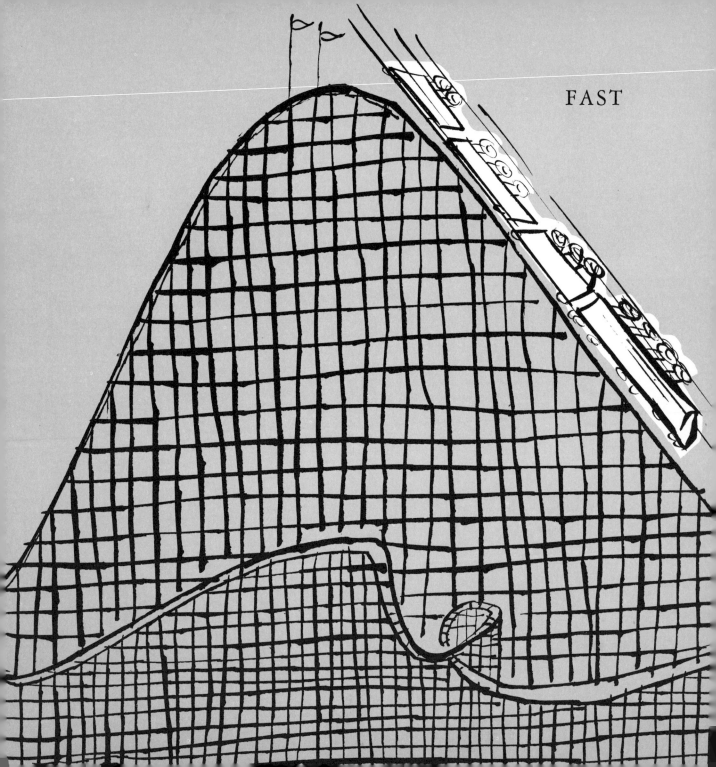

FAST

SLOW

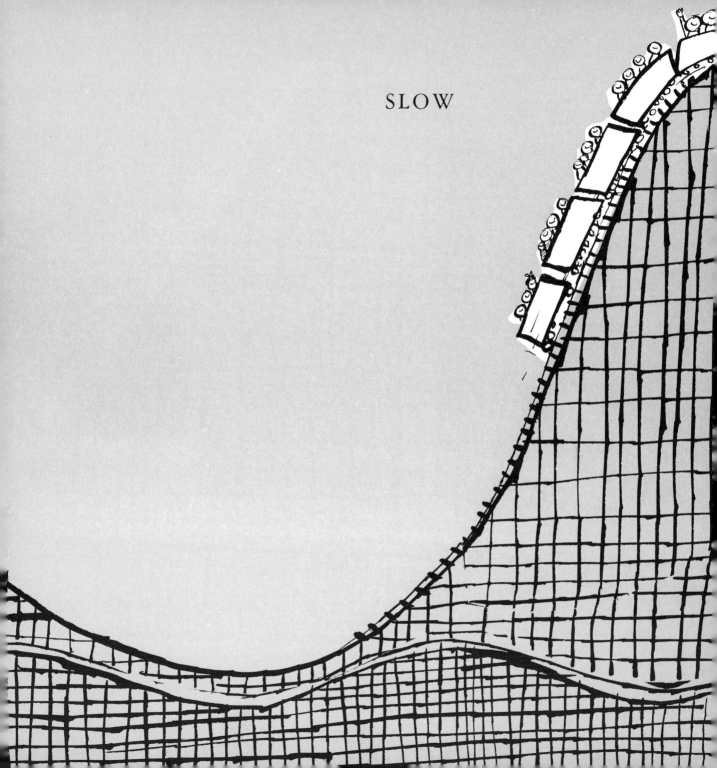

FAST
Is Not A Ladybug

A BOOK ABOUT FAST AND SLOW THINGS

BY MIRIAM SCHLEIN

Illustrated by

LEONARD KESSLER

YOUNG SCOTT BOOKS

Text Copyright © MCMLIII by Miriam Schlein
All Rights Reserved
A Young Scott Book
Addison-Wesley Publishing Company, Inc.
Reading, Massachusetts 01867
Library of Congress Catalog Card Number 53–7805
ISBN: 0–201–09181–X
Printed in the United States of America

HA/BP   09181   8/74

FAST is not a ladybug
crawling on a leaf.
That is SLOW.

What is fast?

Fast is like
a galloping horse,
a bunny,
an airplane,
a speedboat.

Some things in the world just must be fast—
they can't be slow,
because fast is the way they have to go.

Like a ball, when you throw it.

Or a fire engine, racing to a fire.

What does fast mean?
Fast means it takes
less time
to go from here to there.

Do *you* run fast?

But look, the dog runs faster than you.

And the horse runs faster than the dog.

And the train on the track
goes faster than the horse,
that runs faster than the dog,
that runs faster than you.

And a plane in the sky goes even faster
than the train,
that goes faster than the horse,
that runs faster than the dog,
that runs faster than you.

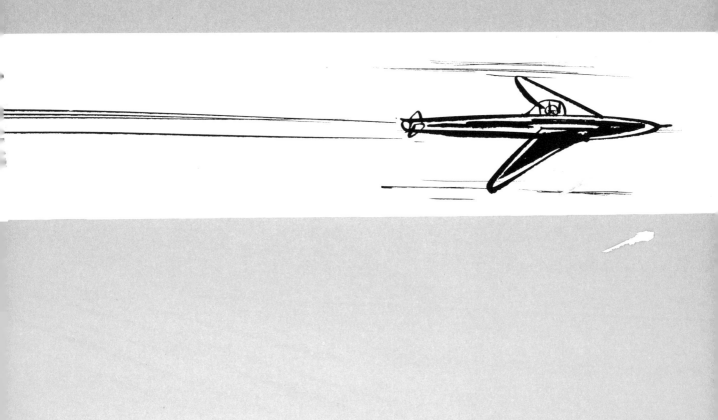
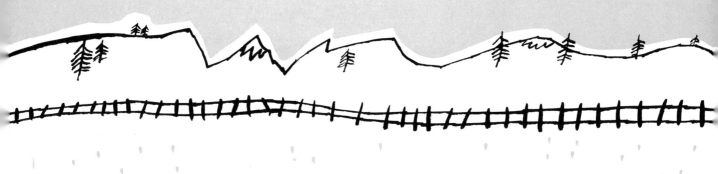

And when a rocket ship
shoots to the moon,
that rocket ship will be even faster
than the plane,
that is faster than the train,
that is faster than the horse,
that is faster than the dog,
that runs faster than you.

And when a rocket ship
shoots to the moon,
it will never be as fast
as a flash of lightning,
that zips through the sky.
Because lightning is the fastest thing
you can see in the whole world,
and that is fast!

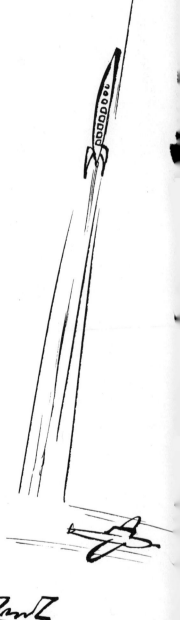

LIGHTNING
ROCKET SHIP
PLANE
TRAIN
HORSE
DOG
YOU

Do you still think you run fast?

Yes, you do!

Just because all these
things are faster than you,
that doesn't mean you're slow.

No! You are not slow at all!

Because even if the horse
runs faster than you,
it is *easier* for a horse
to run faster than you,
and so, for *you,*
you still run fast.
You run as fast as *you* can run—
and that is fast, too!

But look! Here is the ladybug.
She is still walking across that leaf.
Oh, my, she is slow!

Maybe she just
feels like going slow.
If she felt like
going fast,
she would fly.

There are some things
that never even *try* to be fast.

They are slow things—nice and slow.
Slow is the way they always go—

slow as the stars
coming out at night,

slow as you breathe
when you're sleeping,

slow as a cloud
on a lazy day,

slow as a snail
taking a walk.

Oh, how slow!

What does slow mean?
Slow means it takes *more* time
to go from here to there.

It takes a snail
three hundred and ninety-eight hours
to go one mile!

It would take you
less than one hour to walk a mile.

Could you ever take a walk with a snail?
No! You would be miles ahead of him.
Because a snail is very slow.

Once there was a seed,

and a little girl buried the seed

in the dirt.  And slowly,

very slowly,

there came to be a rose bush that

grew up from that little seed.

And a beautiful rose

came to grow on that rose bush,

slowly, very slowly. And the

beautiful rose had petals

that unfolded, slowly,

one by one.

And that was a very slow story,
because growing is always slow.

Look at you.
You used to be a baby.
But you grew, slowly,
a little each day—
you couldn't see it happening—
but very slowly,
bit by bit,
in the sleep of the night
and the smile of the day,
you kept on growing.
And now look how big you are!

This couldn't happen to you
boom, all at once.
Because growing must be slow.

Some things are nice when they're slow.
Some things are nice when they're fast.

It's fun to go fast, sometimes.
But lots of times
I like to know
I can just go slow.

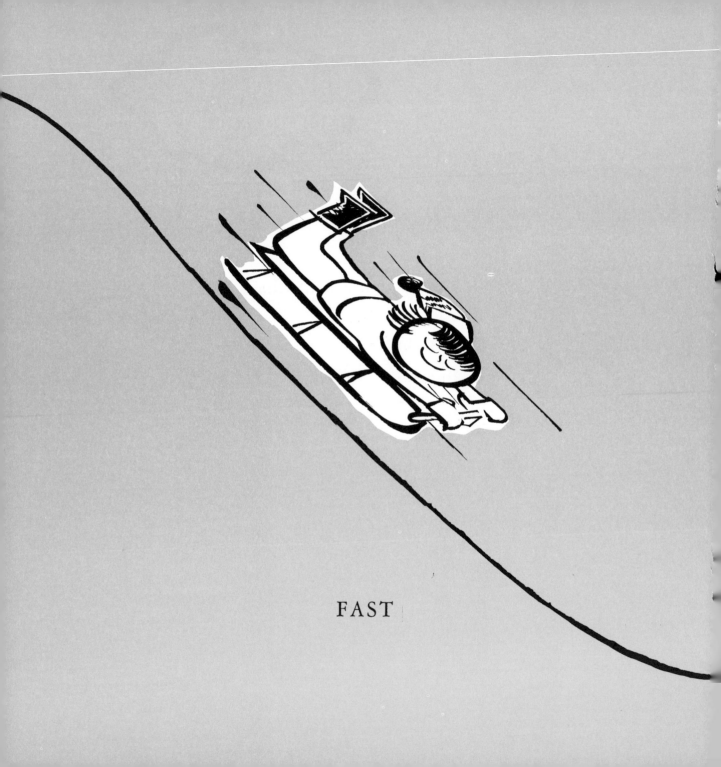

FAST

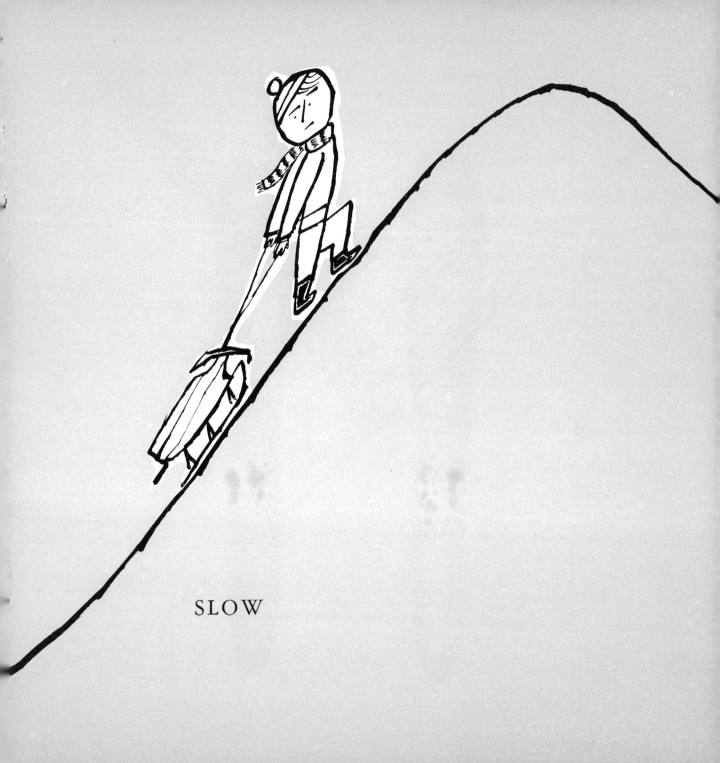

SLOW

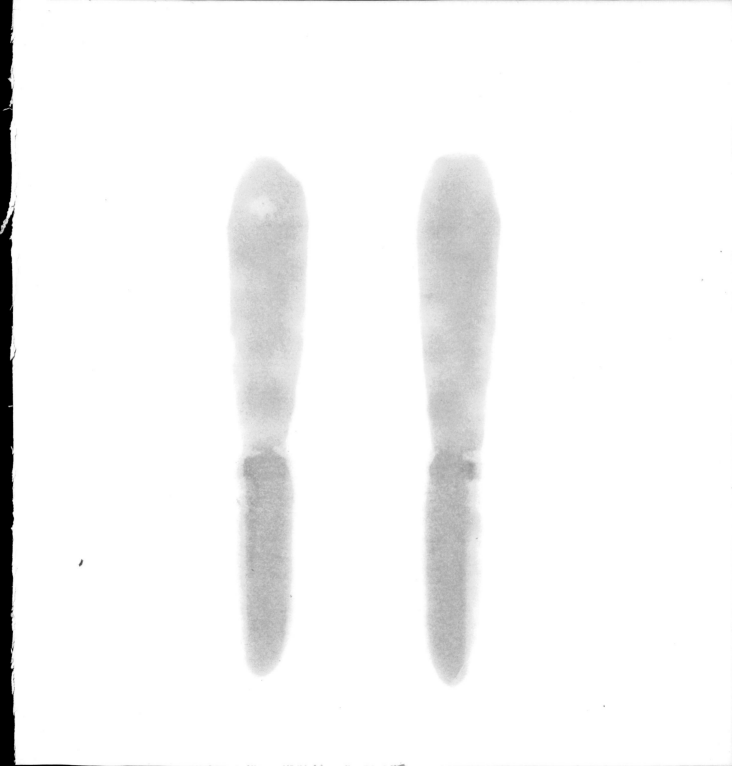

Signs of Jays

By

Linda Kurtz Kingsley

JASON & NORDIC PUBLISHERS
HOLLIDAYSBURG, PENNSYLVANIA

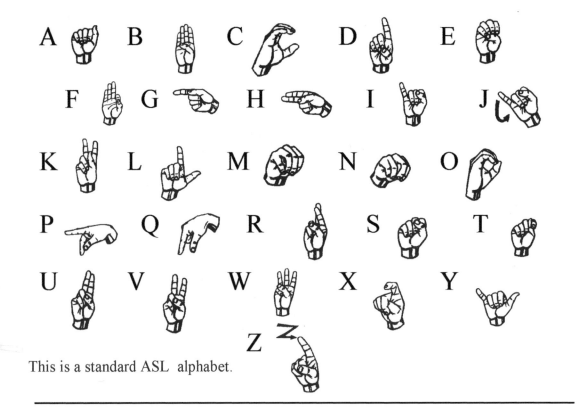

This is a standard ASL alphabet.

Text and Illustrations Copyright© 2008 Linda Kurtz Kingley

ISBN 978-0-944727-22-5 Library Control Number: 2008925612
ISBN 978-0-944727-23-2 :
                    Library of Congress Cataloging-in-Publication Data
Kingsley, Linda Kurtz.
  Signs of jays / by Linda Kurtz Kingsley.
      p. cm.
  Summary: As the children in his mother's class for the hearing impaired prepare to mainstream into classes with hearing students, Pete cares for two injured scrub jays and helps the birds "mainstream" back into the wild.
   ISBN 978-0-944727-23-2 (alk. paper)
 [1. Jays--Fiction. 2. Wildlife rescue--Fiction. 3. Mainstreaming in education--Fiction. 4. Deaf--Fiction. 5. People with disabilities--Fiction.] I. Title.
 PZ7.K6155Si 2008
 [E]--dc22

                              2008022761

Paper: EAN 978-0-944727-22-5
Hardbound: EAN 978-0-944727-23-2

Printed in the United States of America on acid free paper

For:

> Jesse, my son who helped me a lot with the computer aspects of this book and for Sasha, my daughter.

Also many thanks to Norma.

bird

"What have you got there, Uncle Steve?" I asked.

"Two scrub jays, Pete. I had to move their nest when I put in the new rain gutter. Their mother didn't come back to feed them," he said.

"May we keep them?"

"Let's ask your mom," Uncle Steve answered.

two

4

dog

Mom called the wildlife shelter for advice. They told her to stuff little balls of dog food and vitamins into the baby jays' bills every two hours.

food

Monday

On Monday, the jays came with us to school. We took them to Mom's class. She teaches kids who are hearing impaired. They talk with their hands. Using signs, Mom told her class that they would take care of the birds. At night, the birds would come home with us. Then I went to my class.

worm

At recess, Mom brought
the jays to the playground.
We fed the jays worms.
Mike, who's deaf, showed me the sign for
worm.

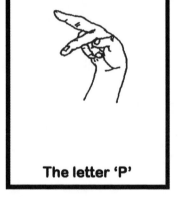

The letter 'P'

Then he gave me my
own name sign: Pete who
likes birds. He made the letter 'p' on his
mouth. Mike and I were friends.

sandwich

Every day, the jays got bigger and hungrier. At lunch they hopped around like windup toys and pecked leftover sandwich crumbs. They liked our plastic cups.

Some of Mike's class and mine squeezed together at the picnic table with the birds in the middle. Our bodies made a fence so the birds couldn't escape.

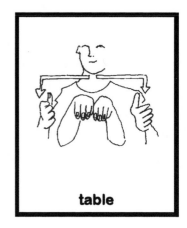

table

pig

skinny

On Friday, the two jay brothers got names. Piggy liked to eat. Skinny-dip liked baths.

At recess and lunch, the kids in Mike's class tried talking and my class tried signs so we could talk together about the jays.

Mike and I helped everyone because he speaks well and I know a lot of signs.

That night at home, the jays started to flutter their wings. Soon they were flying all over our apart-ment. They crashed into walls, pooped on our heads, and got into everything.

night

"It's time they learn to live outside," said Mom. "They need to learn to take

home

care of themselves. We'll have to take them to the wildlife shelter. They can't come to school, and they can't stay here."

teach

"Can't you teach them, Mom?" I asked. "You teach kids every day!"

"Maybe," said Mom. "We could train our birds to live outside a little at a time until they're ready to do it on their own. We can try."

you

box

Mom's class planted flowers in a flower box.

That weekend, we put it on a windowsill inside my room. We added bird food and kept the window open so the jays could go out.

First, the birds just ate their food. Then Piggy cocked his head when he saw another bird and took off. A few minutes later, Skinny-dip did the same thing.

At school I told about it in words and signs.

flower

Every day, Piggy and
Skinny-dip flew outside a
little longer and ate less of
our food. They were finding

world

things to eat outside instead.

When they came home at night, we
shut the window. Mom said we were

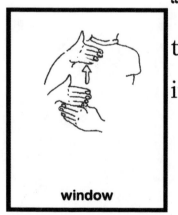

window

"mainstreaming" our jays—
teaching them to get along
in the real world.

cry

One night, the birds didn't come home at all. We kept the window open even though it was cold. Finally, we closed it. I cried, but Mom said we should be happy because the jays are wild and belong outside. She said we had done a good job.

"Maybe we'll see them when winter comes and food is scarce," she said.

school

School ended.

All summer Mike
and I watched out my
window and wondered if
the jays we saw were
ours. We could never tell.

summer

They all looked the same. Sometimes
one cocked its head like Piggy or
splashed in a puddle like Skinny-dip,
and we were almost sure it was them.

warm

It was time for school again and Mike joined my class with an interpreter who signed the teacher's words. Mom said he was ready to be mainstreamed.

It was still warm enough to sit outside for lunch. Mike and I ate in a hurry. I left half my sandwich on the bench, and we raced to the swings.

Like, same as

That's when we saw them: Two big, beautiful scrub jay brothers perched on the bench, eating my crusts and cocking their heads.

We watched those two scrub jays at home in the world, just like us.

DICTIONARY

bird
Index finger and thumb make a beak at the mouth.

box
With both hands show the four sides of a box by aligning parallel hands to indicate width and height.

cry
Use fists with index fingers protruding to mime tears falling from eyes. Be sad.

dog
Right hand clicks thumb and index finger as to call a dog, then slaps hip.

flower
With tips of four fingers mime smelling a flower at both nostrils.

food
Both hands move toward the mouth as to put food in it.

home
where you eat and sleep. Right hand feeds mouth then opens flat to side of head as on pillow.

like, same as
Using the letter Y sign, move back and forth

Monday
The letter M makes a circular clockwise movement.

night
Right hand moves toward and rests on left bent arm at hand to show the sun setting.

the letter P
Place thumb between index finger and next finger. Bend the wrist.

pig
Hand under the chin bends at the knuckles.

sandwich
Place flat palms together. Bend wrist towards right hand. Bring to mouth like a sandwich.

school
Clap hands twice like a teacher calling attention.

skinny
Pinky fingers touch tipsand move away vertically.

summer
With index finger at left brow, bend it and wipe across forehead as if removing perspiration.

table
Use open hands to mime the top and legs of a table.

teach
Put thumbs behind fingers. Place hands at forehead and move out several times.

two
Two fingers are held up, palm facing away from body.

you
Point the index finger out. For plural move from left to right.

warm
Put closed hand, palm up, in front of mouth. Move it up a bit and slowly open it.

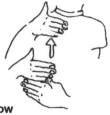

window
Place open hands, palms toward body, on top of each other. Lift top hand to show opening window.

world
Place W hands on top of each other. Top hand circles and returns to beginning place.

worm
Right index finger mimes a worm wiggling across open flat left palm.